LEBRON JAMES
NBA CHAMPION

JUSTINE CIOVACCO

Britannica
Educational Publishing

IN ASSOCIATION WITH

ROSEN
EDUCATIONAL SERVICES

Published in 2016 by Britannica Educational Publishing (a trademark of Encyclopædia Britannica, Inc.) in association with The Rosen Publishing Group, Inc.
29 East 21st Street, New York, NY 10010

Distributed exclusively by Rosen Publishing.
To see additional Britannica Educational Publishing titles, go to rosenpublishing.com.

First Edition

Britannica Educational Publishing
J. E. Luebering: Director, Core Reference Group
Anthony L. Green: Editor, Compton's by Britannica

Rosen Publishing
Hope Lourie Killcoyne: Executive Editor
Tracey Baptiste: Editor
Nelson Sá: Art Director
Nicole Russo: Designer
Cindy Reiman: Photography Manager
Karen Huang: Photo Researcher

Library of Congress Cataloging-in-Publication Data

Ciovacco, Justine.
LeBron James : NBA champion / Justine Ciovacco.
        pages cm.—(Living legends of sports)
Includes bibliographical references and index.
ISBN 978-1-68048-104-4 (library bound) — ISBN 978-1-68048-105-1 (pbk.) — ISBN 978-1-68048-107-5 (6-pack)
1. James, LeBron—Juvenile literature. 2. Basketball players—United States—Biography--Juvenile literature. 3. African American basketball players—Biography—Juvenile literature. I. Title.
GV884.J36C56 2015
796.323092--dc23
[B]

2014039770

Manufactured in the United States of America

Cover, pp. 1, 37, 38 Jason Miller/Getty Images; p. 4 David E. Klutho/Sports Illustrated/Getty Images; p. 7 Johnny Nunez/WireImage/Getty Images; pp. 8, 12 Sporting News Archive/Getty Images; pp. 10–11 John W. McDonough/Sports Illustrated/Getty Images; pp. 13, 16–17, 18–19, 22–23, 24–25, 27, 28-29, 30, 32, 34, 35, 40–41 © AP Images; pp. 20–21 Filippo Monteforte/AFP/Getty Images; cover and interior pages background images © iStockphoto.com/block37 (basketball court illustration), © iStockphoto.com/Nikada (texture).

CONTENTS

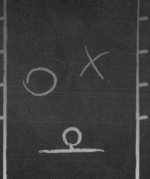

INTRO-DUCTION

LeBron James is one of those rare professional sports stars who is exciting to watch, always improving his game, and eager to be a good role model. He has learned the pressure and the power that come with his role as a living legend. James knows what it's like to be one of the most popular players on the court and to attract massive amounts of attention from the media and fans alike. He also knows what it's like to have fans and media turn against him.

James earned the nickname King James as a young player, before he was drafted into the National Basketball Association (NBA) right after high school. He became the youngest player in NBA history to reach many amazing goals, including winning the Rookie of the Year award and scoring 10,000 career points.

LeBron James shoots against the Chicago Bulls in 2014.

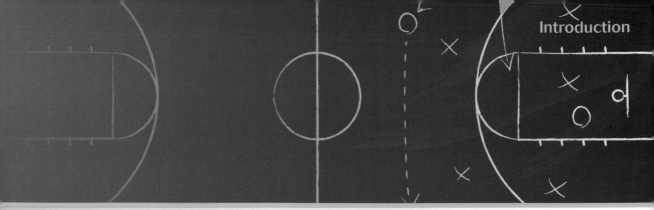

All eyes have been on him from his humble start as a forward with the Cleveland Cavaliers to the media frenzy that followed his shocking move to the Miami Heat, where he won two championships (2012 and 2013). The move—and the way the popular star chose to make his announcement—taught fans and LeBron himself some difficult lessons.

LeBron's decision to return to his hometown team in 2014 also focused the spotlight on him. His move back to Cleveland highlighted the importance of team loyalty and the love of just playing the game—not just playing to win.

CHAPTER ONE

Early Life in Ohio

LeBron James's early life was sometimes difficult. But he had the support of family and friends who wanted the best for him. LeBron turned this good luck into relationships that helped him through an intense start to his career.

Growing Up

LeBron Raymone James was born on December 30, 1984, in Akron, Ohio. His mother, Gloria, was only sixteen at the time of his birth, and she would raise her only child alone. LeBron never met his father. It was difficult for Gloria to work and look after her young son. She didn't have much help because her mom died three years after LeBron was born. Her mother's death meant she also had to care for her two younger brothers.

LeBron and his mom, Gloria, have always had a warm relationship. They are pictured together here in 2009.

Gloria, her brothers, and LeBron moved a lot and lived in rough neighborhoods while Gloria tried to find steady jobs. They moved twelve times when LeBron was between the ages of five and eight. The moves meant LeBron had to get adjusted to new schools and make new friends each time. His young life was not stable and he would sometimes miss school. He missed 82 days out of 160 in fourth grade.

LeBron had a hard time growing up without a father, and the many moves made him feel frustrated. His mother was loving but busy making ends meet. His uncles were great company, but they were much older so they had their own friends. LeBron spent a lot of time riding his bike, just trying to stay out of trouble.

LeBron's basketball skills were clear even as a high school student. Here, he takes control of the ball for St. Vincent-St. Mary High School in 2003.

Focusing His Energy on Sports

In school, LeBron put his energy into football and basketball. Through sports he found confidence and friends. In fourth grade, he met Frankie Walker Jr., Sian Cotton, Dru Joyce III, and Willie McGee—who all became his lifelong friends. These relationships taught LeBron that loyalty to and from friends and family is one of the keys to happiness and success.

LeBron was always faster and stronger than other kids, which made him stand out in football and basketball. His friend Frankie's father, Frankie Sr., saw his talent and knew he missed a lot of school. He asked Gloria if LeBron could live with him and his wife, Pam, for a short time so they could help give him a more stable life. Gloria worried about this, but she agreed because she wanted LeBron to have what he needed to do well in life.

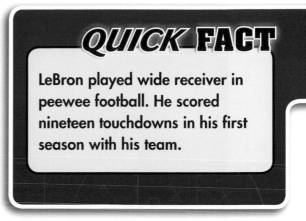

QUICK FACT

LeBron played wide receiver in peewee football. He scored nineteen touchdowns in his first season with his team.

LeBron moved in with the Walkers in fifth grade. His stable home was now shaped by Frankie Sr. and Pam, as well as his friend Frankie and Frankie's sisters Chanelle and Tanesha. The kids had chores and their homework was checked. LeBron's attendance and grades at school improved. The next year, he moved back with his mom, but he still spent a lot of time with the Walkers.

Frankie Sr. also taught LeBron about basketball. LeBron and his four friends joined an Amateur Athletic Union (AAU) team while in middle school. The Fab Five, as they called themselves, traveled to tournaments and had fun playing the game they loved as part of the Northeast Ohio Shooting Stars. They also won big, racking up more than 200 wins.

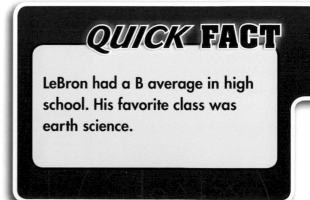

QUICK FACT

LeBron had a B average in high school. His favorite class was earth science.

LeBron makes a layup to bring his high school team closer to victory at the Dream Classic championship game versus a Los Angeles team in 2003.

LeBron was always strong in sports, but he became a star player after he learned about team-work—at home and in the game. When it came time to choose a high school, LeBron and his friends decided to stick together so they could play on the same team.

They chose St. Vincent-St. Mary High School in Akron. In their freshman season, they led the boys' basketball team to a 27–0 record and the Division III state title. LeBron averaged 18 points and six rebounds per game.

Sophomore year was also a success. As a forward, LeBron led his team to a 26–1 record and another Division III title. He averaged 25.2 points, 7.2 rebounds, 5.8 assists, and 3.8 steals that season. The team placed fifth in USA Today's Super 25 high school rankings. LeBron became the youngest player ever to be chosen for the newspaper's All-USA First Team of all-stars, and a local newspaper nicknamed the sixteen-year-old "King James."

LeBron stayed humble and focused on his role within a great team. "It didn't matter if the opposing team was bigger than us or taller than us," he told *Sports Illustrated*. "We knew we had the ability to go out and win every night because we played as a team."

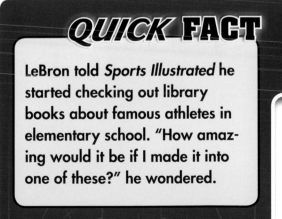

QUICK FACT

LeBron told *Sports Illustrated* he started checking out library books about famous athletes in elementary school. "How amazing would it be if I made it into one of these?" he wondered.

In his junior year, LeBron led his team to a 23–4 record. That season (2001–2002) brought a few more losses than previous years, but he averaged 29 points,

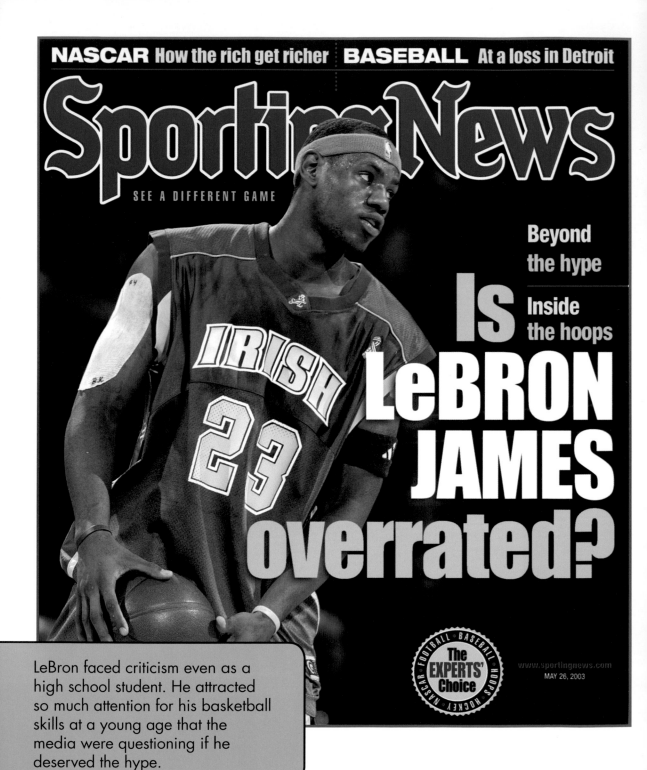

NASCAR How the rich get richer BASEBALL At a loss in Detroit

Sporting News

SEE A DIFFERENT GAME

Beyond
the hype

Inside
the hoops

Is LeBRON JAMES overrated?

IRISH 23

The EXPERTS' Choice

FOOTBALL · BASEBALL · HOOPS · HOCKEY · NASCAR

www.sportingnews.com
MAY 26, 2003

LeBron faced criticism even as a high school student. He attracted so much attention for his basketball skills at a young age that the media were questioning if he deserved the hype.

8.3 rebounds, 5.7 assists, and 3.3 steals per game. St. Vincent-St. Mary lost the state championship in the final game.

Still, attention on LeBron was building. National media was covering his games and fans started devoting websites to him. People were comparing him to his idol, Michael Jordan of the Chicago Bulls. Amazingly, he made the cover of *Sports Illustrated* at age seventeen in his junior season.

Crowds were eager to see him in action. His school moved home games from their gym to the University of Akron's JAR Arena, which holds 6,000 people. The games were sellouts and became a hit on pay-per-view TV, too. ESPN even televised some of the games as interest in LeBron grew.

QUICK FACT

In his junior year, LeBron led his football team to the state semifinals, but he broke the index finger on his left hand just before the start of basketball season. That didn't stop him from playing.

Gatorade named LeBron as its male National Athlete of the Year in 2003. Here, he enjoys the attention at a ceremony honoring him and his fellow honoree, sprinter Allyson Felix.

Senior year proved to be a good one for LeBron—and his growing number of fans. His team's record was 25–1, and they won their third state title in four years. LeBron averaged 31.6 points, 9.6 rebounds, 4.6 assists, and 3.4 steals.

LeBron's personal life was going well, too. He was living with his mom in an apartment in Akron. It was a gathering place for all of his friends—a comfortable spot where they could goof around and play video games. He believes his friends made his apartment their usual spot because they loved his mom, but his friends were also eager just to be wherever he was. "[It was] his charisma," explains his long-time friend Randy Mims, who now serves as the basketball star's day-to-day manager. "Everyone wanted to be around him. He was born with it. He still has it."

However, senior year would also bring the need to consider change. Would LeBron choose to fine-tune his skills in college, or move onto his dream job with the NBA? LeBron was confident that he was ready for something much bigger.

Becoming One of the Best in the NBA

Although James was a basketball star early on, he didn't always have the wins he was used to in his high school days. That sometimes proved a disappointment for both James and his fans.

Into the NBA

James's basketball skills made him famous in high school, and he was ready to achieve more. On April 25, 2003, LeBron announced that he would be part of the NBA Draft for the 2003–2004 NBA season.

The news created excitement around the country. Many teams were eager to take him in his rookie year, but the first to pick was the luckiest. And the first pick went to the Cleveland Cavaliers.

James proudly holds up his number 23 Cleveland Cavaliers jersey at a press conference on June 27, 2003. He chose the same number as his idol Michael Jordan.

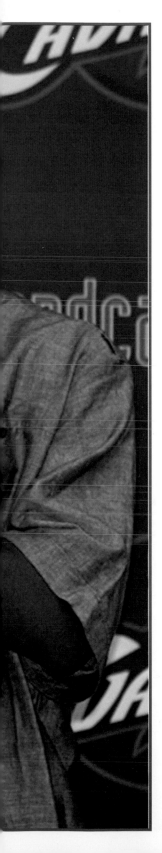

QUICK FACT

Nike signed James to a $90 million seven-year contract days before he was drafted to the Cavaliers.

"With the first pick of the 2003 NBA Draft," NBA commissioner David Stern announced during the ceremony, "the Cleveland Cavaliers select LeBron James!" Cavaliers fans cheered the pick; some even danced in the streets. They knew James was the best young player in the country. Fans immediately began buying James's number 23 jersey.

At that time, the Cavaliers were one of the worst teams in the NBA. They had won only seventeen games in the 2002–2003 season. That didn't matter to James. He had been a huge fan of the team since he was a kid in nearby Akron. He understood it would take a lot of work for the team to get on track, and he was confident he could help. Plus, James was excited to train close to home and his friends.

"I'm one of the highest publicized players in the country right now, and I haven't even played one game of basketball in the NBA," James admitted. "I know I'm a marked man, but I just have to go out there and play hard and play strong and help my teammates every night."

As a rookie player, James felt pressure to prove that he deserved his NBA contract. The 6-foot-8-inch star was such a powerhouse that he quickly became the team's top scorer.

QUICK FACT

In 2005, twenty-year-old James became the youngest player to score fifty points in a game. His record was beaten in 2009 by Brandon Jennings of the Milwaukee Bucks, who was twenty-eight days younger when he made history.

James signed a three-year contract for $10.8 million. From the start, he led the team in scoring, steals, and minutes played per game. He helped the team boost their wins to thirty-five for the 2003–2004 season. His influence was so big that he was voted NBA Rookie of the Year. That meant everything to James. His hero Michael Jordan had also gotten the honor back in 1985.

James followed up with a spot on the U.S. basketball team at the 2004 Olympics in Athens, Greece. The nineteen-year-old was the team's youngest player. Among his teammates was Dwayne Wade, who played for the Miami Heat.

Team USA players (*left to right*) Michael Redd, Deron Williams, LeBron James, Jason Kidd, and Carlos Boozer celebrate their 2008 Olympic win against Spain.

Sports fans expected the team to win gold and were disappointed when they came home with third-place bronze medals. James felt like he let people down and he wasn't going to let that happen again when

he returned with the U.S. team at the 2008 Olympics in Beijing, China. There, he teamed up with Wade again, as well as Chris Bosh (Toronto Raptors) and Kobe Bryant (Los Angeles Lakers), among other greats.

QUICK FACT

James was picked for the NBA All-Star team in 2004–2005, even though the Cavs didn't make the play-offs.

This time the team took home the gold.

James had already become a father at this point in his life. His girlfriend since high school, Savannah Brinson, gave birth to son LeBron Jr. in October 2004. The couple's second son, Bryce Maximus, was born in June 2007.

James's Frustration Builds

Back on the court in Cleveland, James was disappointed that the Cavaliers didn't make the play-offs in his first two years on the team. As a result, he didn't get along well with coach Paul Silas. When Silas was fired in 2005, fans and critics blamed James.

James stayed focused on making the play-offs. He averaged 30 points per game for the 2005–2006 season. The Cavaliers reached

Bryce (*left*) and LeBron Jr. stand by their dad as James receives his fourth Most Valuable Player Award from the NBA in 2013.

the play-offs for the first time in eight years but lost in the Eastern Conference finals to the Detroit Pistons.

They made the play-offs again in 2007. This time they made it to the NBA Finals, but the San Antonio Spurs swept them in four games.

By 2010, James was frustrated with his team, and Cleveland Cavaliers fans were not happy that his attitude and performance showed it.

James was still eager to work with the Cavaliers and signed a three-year, $60-million contract extension, giving him an option for a fourth year. He could have signed a longer contract for more money, but

James wanted to become an unrestricted free agent after the 2009–2010 season. He knew that would allow him the freedom to join any team he wanted, and he had discussed his plan with pals Dwayne Wade and Chris Bosh, who also planned to become free agents in 2010.

In 2008 it was the Boston Celtics's turn to knock the Cavaliers out of the play-offs. In 2009, Cleveland lost the Eastern Conference finals to the Orlando Magic in six games. James was angry, and he left the court without shaking his opponents' hands. Critics and fans noticed.

James's eagerness to win and frustration with play-off losses increased each year. In the 2010 play-offs, the Cavs lost to the Celtics in Game 6. Many fans and critics were angry with LeBron, who seemed to give up by Game 5, in which he only scored 15 points. Fans booed as he left the court.

CHAPTER THREE

King James Moves to Miami

Despite the losses, James was still a basketball star. He used his celebrity and his money to help kids in his hometown. But eventually, he wanted to move on with his career. His decision to leave Cleveland for another team was met with anger from some, and joy from others.

Being a Role Model

Even as a rookie, James was happy to give back to fans and his hometown. Every Thanksgiving when he played for the Cavs, he and his friends would hand out turkeys and bags of groceries to families who needed them most. Each summer for five years, he gave away AK-Rowdy bikes to 300 needy children and then rode with them in downtown Akron. He even established a bike repair program where kids could go for repairs. He often gave money and his time to local groups and events. James was a thoughtful role model. He always took that part of his job

James poses with kids from the Boys and Girls Club of Central Florida in 2012. Through his foundation, corporate sponsors donated sports equipment and renovated their baseball field and picnic area.

seriously—just as seriously as he took his sport. Fans respected his home-town love and were proud to have a world-class player on their team.

The Decision

Still, by 2010 James was growing frustrated with the Cavaliers' management and the team's inability to win a championship. James's contract with the Cavs expired on July 1, 2010, and he became a free agent. He took meetings with many NBA teams, including the Los Angeles Clippers, the New York Knicks, the Chicago Bulls, and the Miami Heat.

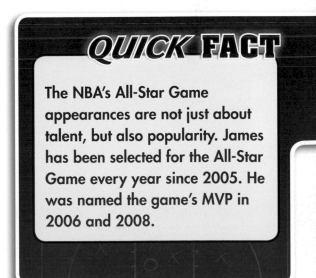

QUICK FACT

The NBA's All-Star Game appearances are not just about talent, but also popularity. James has been selected for the All-Star Game every year since 2005. He was named the game's MVP in 2006 and 2008.

Fans wait outside the Boys and Girls Club of Greenwich, Connecticut, to greet James before his big announcement on July 8, 2010.

On July 6, news broke that James had made a decision on where he'd continue his career. He would announce it in an hour-long live TV special on ESPN called, "The Decision." The media and fans were filled with excitement about what he would say. James had the full attention of the sports world.

On July 7 and the morning of the eigth, LeBron's attention was in Akron, as he was holding his annual Nike camp for the country's top high school and college players. On the seventh, he also joined the social media site Twitter, something he had said in the past he would never do because he saw it as a distraction from the game. His website was also redesigned. These moves were signs to many that James wanted the spotlight, not just as a player, but as an attention-grabbing legend.

On July 8th, James flew to a Boys and Girls Club in Greenwich, Connecticut, for the live event. The media was so focused on James's announcement that little attention was given to a noon press conference in which his friends Dwayne Wade and Chris Bosh announced they were signing contracts with the Miami Heat.

Halfway through his TV special, James announced, "I'm taking my talents to South Beach [Miami]." James said he couldn't focus on Cleveland fans who would be upset. "I wanted to do what was best for LeBron James," he said. "At the end of the day, I feel awful. I feel even worse that I wasn't able to bring an NBA championship to that city." He added that he felt "the greatest challenge for me, is to move on."

Fans watching the announcement at downtown Cleveland bars and restaurants took to the streets to show their anger. They set fire to number 23 jerseys and threw rocks at a billboard of the star player. Cavs owner Dan Gilbert added to the rage when he posted a letter to fans on the team's website. "As you now know, our former hero, who grew up in the very region that he deserted this evening, is no longer a Cleveland Cavalier," he wrote. "This was announced with a several day, narcissistic,

A fan in Cleveland shows what he thinks of James at a December 2010 game between the Cleveland Cavaliers and James's new team, the Miami Heat.

self-promotional build-up [ending] with a national TV special of his 'decision' unlike anything ever 'witnessed' in the history of sports and probably the history of entertainment. Clearly, this is bitterly disappointing to all of us."

Gilbert said James had stopped playing his best for the Cavs in the Finals, and build-up surrounding his announcement added to the pain. James was criticized by many fans and critics for the way he made his announcement. It was promoted as a way to raise $3 million for the Boys and Girls Clubs, but the build-up to the announcement and his words stung many Cavs fans and critics who felt it didn't suit James's humble personality. Fans felt he was disrespectful to the team that gave him a start.

One of sport's most beloved stars became one its most disliked, except in Miami, where he was welcomed with sold-out games. Many former fans and critics wished to see the new Miami Heat fail. That didn't happen.

James returned to Cleveland as a member of the Heat on December 2 and was met with boos every time he touched the ball. Still, he had a great season, with averages of 26.7 points, 7.5 rebounds, and 7 assists per game. He helped Miami reach the NBA Finals, but the team lost the championship to the Dallas Mavericks.

Giving Back to Kids Back Home

James's hometown was still on his mind. In April 2011, he and his LeBron James Family Foundation took on one of their biggest projects. Studies show that third grade is a big year for children. Their reading skills, in particular, are a good indicator for how they will grow into educated adults. Each year, James's foundation began contacting every in-coming third grader in the Akron public school system who was considered at risk, meaning their skills were not at the third grade level or above. The students received an invitation to join James's program, Wheels for Education. "I was the same as them," James told *Sports Illustrated*. "I could have gone either way."

James wanted to help kids in Ohio even when he played for Miami. Here, he and his mom, Gloria, gather with children taking part in his foundation's Wheels for Education program in 2012.

Each year since 2011 between 200 and 300 students have signed up to take part in a two-week camp in fall. At the end, James gives each student an AK-Rowdy bike. He also makes them say the promise:

I promise: To go to school. To do all of my homework. To listen to my teachers because they will help me learn. To ask questions and find answers. To never give up, no matter what. To always try my best. To be helpful and respectful to others. To live a healthy life by eating right and being active. To make good choices for myself. To have fun. And above all else, to finish school!

In return, James and members of his foundation continually check in with students in the program. James also sends them letters and encourages them to read and participate in after-school learning programs. The students stay in contact with James and his staff through high school graduation. The goal is to encourage them to move on to college.

Big Wins in Miami

In the 2011–12 season, James averaged 27.1 points per game and won his third MVP award while helping Miami advance to its second NBA Finals appearance in a row. He was named the Finals MVP after the Heat defeated the Oklahoma City Thunder to win the championship. King James finally had the big win he always wanted.

He had arguably his greatest individual season in 2012–13, when he averaged 26.8 points, 7.3 assists, and a career-high 8.0 rebounds per game. James also helped Miami win 27 games in a row that season. He was rewarded with his fourth NBA MVP award.

QUICK FACT

In 2012, James became only the second player to win an NBA MVP award, NBA championship, NBA Finals MVP, and Olympic gold medal in the same year. The first was his hero, Michael Jordan.

James proudly holds his first championship ring, given to him in Miami on October 30, 2012.

In the postseason, the Heat defeated the San Antonio Spurs in a seven-game series to win the NBA championship again. James was again named the Finals MVP.

Team USA's Kevin Durant, Carmelo Anthony, LeBron James, and Kobe Bryant pose after a gold medal win at the 2012 Summer Olympics in London.

On September 15, 2013, James had a win of a different kind: He married Savannah Brinson, his love since high school. The wedding was part of a three-day party in San Diego, California.

James continued to do well in the 2013–2014 season, even increasing his shooting percentage by .002, and he again led the Heat to the NBA Finals. However, Miami lost the rematch with the Spurs in a five-game series.

QUICK FACT

James won his second Olympic gold medal as part of the U.S. basketball team in 2012. Chris Bosh and Dwayne Wade withdrew from the team due to injuries, but James reteamed with Kobe Bryant.

The Return to Ohio

James achieved his goal of winning a championship. Now that he was a free agent, he had the opportunity to go anywhere he wanted. Several teams were still interested in him. Fans waited to see what he would do next.

QUICK FACT

In 2013, James paid for a redesign of his old high school gym. A sentence painted on the wall of the new training room is one of his quotes: "I promise to never forget where I came from."

"I'm Coming Home"

After the Finals loss in Miami, James felt ready to make another big career move and another big announcement. In a week of excited speculation among fans and the media, it was reported that James talked with the Cavaliers, Houston Rockets, Los Angeles Lakers, Dallas Mavericks, and Phoenix Suns.

James announced his decision in an essay for *Sports Illustrated*, which was posted online on Friday, July 11, 2014. It was titled, "I'm Coming Home." In the sincere, thoughtful statement, James thanked Heat fans and discussed his love for his home state and why he made his decision.

James explained why he originally left Cleveland and why he wanted to come back to the place where he spent the first seven years of his career:

> When I left Cleveland, I was on a mission. I was seeking championships, and we won two. But Miami already knew that feeling. Our city hasn't had that feeling in a long, long, long time. My goal is still to win as many titles as possible, no question. But what's most important for me is bringing one trophy back to Northeast Ohio.

James's return to the Cavaliers was a thrill for many in Ohio, including these Cleveland Indians baseball fans.

James celebrates with cheering Cavaliers fans after scoring in a November 2014 game.

He also explained how difficult the decision was and how he finally made peace with the past, including Cavaliers owner Dan Gilbert and Cleveland fans:

QUICK **FACT**

James's four NBA MVP honors put him in excellent company. His hero, Michael Jordan, received the title five times, but Kareem Abdul-Jabbar holds the record with six MVP titles.

> *It was easy to say, "OK, I don't want to deal with these people ever again." But then you think about the other side. What if I were a kid who looked up to an athlete, and that athlete made me want to do better in my own life, and then he left? How would I react? I've met with Dan, face-to-face, man-to-man. We've talked it out. Everybody makes mistakes. I've made mistakes as well.*

James explained that another part of the decision had to do with where he and Savannah should bring up their sons and their then-unborn daughter. He said he wanted to show them "there's no better place to grow up." "In northeast Ohio, nothing is given," he noted. "You work for what you have."

James's announcement was the lead news story, not just on sports websites and sports TV channels but also on many national and local newscasts. Heat fans were disappointed, but Cleveland fans were running joyfully through downtown Cleveland. Season tickets were sold out in ten hours. LeBron's website crashed when too many fans tried to access it at once.

James signed a two-year contract worth $42 million, and many sports fans felt he was worth every penny. It wasn't just LeBron's status as one of the best players in the NBA that excited fans; it was his decision to work hard with the young but talented team. He said he looked forward to working with and mentoring the team.

James's focus, when not playing the game he loves, is on his family. He is seen here with sons LeBron Jr. (*left*) and Bryce at an NBA All-Star event in 2012.

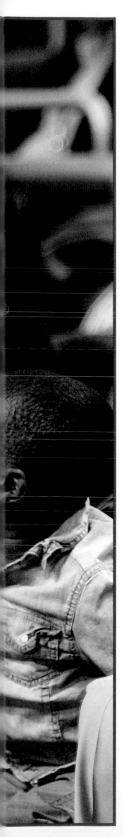

"I'm the biggest figure that my hometown has ever seen," James told *Gentleman's Quarterly* in 2014. "The responsibility of being the inspiration and the light for my community— it's much greater than hitting a jump-shot."

James's family and friends in Ohio are thrilled James, Savannah, and their children are back full-time living in the Akron area. Just like their first two children, the couple's third was born in Ohio—and at a time when their father was a member of the Cavaliers. Zhuri Nova James was born in October 2014, and her dad was looking forward to what life with a daughter would be like. "You give rough love to your boys and you give soft love to your daughter," he explained to the Associated Press.

LeBron James has a lot more to look forward to as he continues his career with the Cavaliers. His playing style, hard work, and team spirit have made him a favorite among players and fans. He is also admired for his ability to be a humble star and a focused family man. After all, what matters most to James is what got him where he is today: his love of the game and his close relationships with friends and family.

QUICK FACT

Colleges started sending basketball scholarship offers to LeBron's oldest son, LeBron Jr., when he was just ten years old. James didn't like it. "Let him be a kid," he said.

TIMELINE

1984 LeBron Raymone James is born on December 30 in Akron, Ohio.

1997 James joins the Amateur Athletic Union team, the Northeast Ohio Shooting Stars.

2000 High school freshman James leads Saint Vincent-Saint Mary High School to the Ohio state basketball championship.

2001 Sophomore James leads his school to a second state title.

2003 Senior James leads his school to a third state title. He is drafted into the NBA by the Cleveland Cavaliers.

2004 James is named Rookie of the Year. His son LeBron Jr. is born.

2007 The Cavaliers reach the NBA Finals for the first time. James's son Bryce Maximus is born.

2008 James becomes the youngest player and fastest ever to reach the following NBA milestones: 10,000 points, 2,500 rebounds, 2,500 assists, 700 steals, and 300 blocks. He leads the NBA in scoring, and wins a gold medal at the Olympics in Beijing.

2009 James wins first NBA MVP Award, receiving it at the gym at St. Vincent-St. Mary.

2010 James wins his second NBA MVP Award. On July 8, he announces he's joining the Miami Heat.

2011 James becomes the seventh player in NBA history to record seven consecutive 2,000 point seasons. The Heat lose in the finals. His Wheels for Education program begins.

2012 James receives his third NBA MVP award, and the Heat win the NBA championship. He wins a second gold medal at the Olympics in London.

2013 James receives his fourth NBA MVP award as the Heat win their second championship. On September 14, he marries Savannah Brinson.

2014 James rejoins the Cavaliers. His daughter, Zhuri, is born.

OTHER LIVING LEGENDS OF BASKETBALL

Kareem Abdul-Jabbar (1947–) played with the Milwaukee Bucks (1969–75) and the Los Angeles Lakers (1975–89). The center was a six-time NBA MVP, a member of six NBA championship teams as a player and two as the Lakers' assistant coach, and was a two-time NBA Finals MVP.

Kobe Bryant (1978–) is the Los Angeles Lakers' all-time leading scorer. He has won five NBA championships, was named NBA Finals MVP twice and NBA MVP once, and won two gold medals with the 2008 and 2012 Olympic teams.

Magic Johnson (1959–) served as the Los Angeles Lakers' point guard (1979–1991, 1996) and as coach (1994). He helped lead the Lakers to five NBA championships, was named NBA Finals MVP and NBA MVP three times each, and won a gold medal with the 1992 Olympic team.

Michael Jordan (1963–) led the Chicago Bulls to six NBA championships. He is a five-time NBA MVP and six-time NBA Finals MVP. He also won two Olympic gold medals as part of Team USA.

Shaquille O'Neal (1972–) played for six NBA teams. He started out with the Orlando Magic, won three NBA championships with the Lakers and one with the Miami Heat, and won a gold medal as part of the 1996 Olympic team. He was a three-time NBA Finals MVP and one-time NBA MVP.

Bill Russell (1934–) played center for the Boston Celtics (1956–1969) and served as a coach for the Celtics, Seattle SuperSonics, and Sacramento Kings. He helped lead the Celtics to eleven championships, won the NBA MVP five times, and was on the gold-medal-winning 1956 Olympic basketball team.

GLOSSARY

contract A legal agreement between people or companies.

critic A person who expresses an opinion about something, especially in sports or the arts.

free agent A professional athlete who is free to sign a contract to play for any team.

marked man Someone who is in danger of harm or criticism by others.

NBA Draft The National Basketball Association's annual event at which professional basketball teams select young players for their teams.

opposing team The team being competed against.

play-offs A series of games played at the end of the regular season that determines which player or team is the champion.

publicize To cause something to be publicly known.

ranking The position in a group.

rebound Catching the ball after a shot has missed going in the basket.

rookie A first-year player in a professional sport.

season The schedule of official games played or to be played by a sports team.

steal Deflecting, controlling, or catching the ball from an opponent and redirecting it to one's own team.

tournament A competition or series of contests that involves many players or teams and usually continues for several days.

train To be taught the skills needed to do something.

Books

Augustyn, Adam. *The Britannica Guide to Basketball*. New York, NY: Rosen Publishing/Britannica 2012.

Burns, Brian. *Skills in Motion: Basketball Step-by-Step*. New York, NY: Rosen Publishing, 2010.

Gage, Christos. *LeBron James: King of the Rings*. New York, NY: Marvel Comics, 2013.

Hill, Anne E. *LeBron James: King of Shots* (USA Lifeline Biographies). Minneapolis, MN: Twenty-First Century Books, 2012.

Hollar, Sherman. *Inside Sports: Basketball and Its Greatest Players*. New York, NY: Rosen Publishing/Britannica, 2012.

Norwich, Grace. *I Am LeBron James*. New York, NY: Scholastic, Inc., 2014.

Ramen, Fred. *Basketball: Rules, Tips, Strategy, and Safety*. New York, NY: Rosen Publishing, 2007.

Websites

Because of the changing nature of Internet links, Rosen Publishing has developed an online list of websites related to the subject of this book. This site is updated regularly. Please use this link to access this list:

http://www.rosenlinks.com/LLS/James

INDEX